Bible Stories & Activities
Jonah

6412 Maple Ave.
Westminster, CA 92683
ISBN: 978-1-4206-7906-9
©2008 Learning Train
Made in U.S.A.

Table of Contents

Introduction

Jonah is a favorite Bible character of many children. Toddlers love the unusual story of Jonah swallowed by a fish! And children as well as adults identify with Jonah's desire to run from God to avoid responsibility.

Unlike many other well-known Bible characters, Jonah's whole story is not told in the Bible. In the four chapters of his book, we learn only what happened to him during a very short period of his life, perhaps a matter of weeks. We know that he was a prophet of God from 800 B.C. to 750 B.C., about the same time as the prophet Amos.

Yet despite this brief encounter, Jonah remains a great source of Biblical inspiration and teaching. Students will enjoy learning about Jonah through puzzles, crafts, action rhymes and songs, word games, and many other fun, creative activities. Most activities require that students use their Bibles to find or check their answers. (**Note:** This book uses the *New International Version* for scripture references.) A complete answer key is provided on pages 47–48 for your convenience.

The book is divided into two stories of Jonah with correlated activities: "Jonah and the Great Fish" and "Jonah Goes to Nineveh." Students will discover for themselves the importance of obedience and faith in God as they see how Jonah tried, unsuccessfully, to run away from Him.

A bulletin board is provided on pages 4 and 5, which can be used throughout the study of Jonah. Some of the activity pages are all about Jonah while others are application activities to help students look at their own relationship with God and other people and discover what God wants them to do. The amazing story of Jonah was included in the Bible not just to inform us about one of God's great men, but to help us learn important truths about obeying and trusting the One who made us and sees everything we do, wherever we are. If we refuse to obey Him, then God sometimes uses some interesting ways to convince us, as Jonah learned.

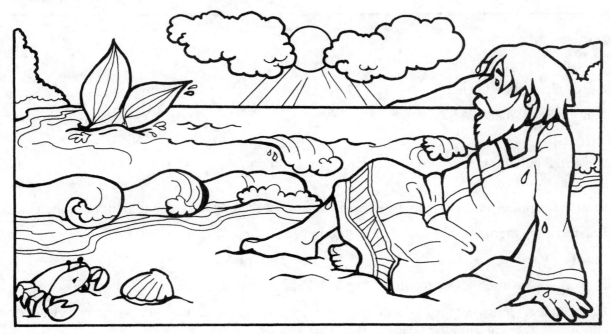

"Jonah" Bulletin Board

Jonah, go preach to Nineveh!

Love your enemies.

Obey your parents.

Be kind to others.

Follow Jesus.

SAY "YES" TO GOD!

Forgive others.

Believe God's Word.

When God tells you what to do, you'd better do it!

Materials

- patterns on page 5
- markers or colored pencils
- light blue and medium blue butcher paper
- white paper
- scissors

Directions

1. Cover the bulletin board with blue butcher paper—light blue above for the sky and medium blue at the bottom for water.

2. Print the captions on strips of white paper and mount them at the top and bottom of the board.

3. Enlarge the patterns of Jonah and the fish on page 5. Color them and cut them out.

4. Put Jonah and the fish in the water.

5. Print God's instructions to Jonah on a speech balloon and attach it at the top of the board.

6. Have students tell what they know God wants them to do. Print their ideas on open Bible shapes and scatter them around the board.

Jonah's Prayer

Directions: From inside the stomach of a fish, Jonah prayed. He confessed his sin and praised God. Use the code to discover some of Jonah's words to God. Look up Jonah 2:6b–7a to check your work.

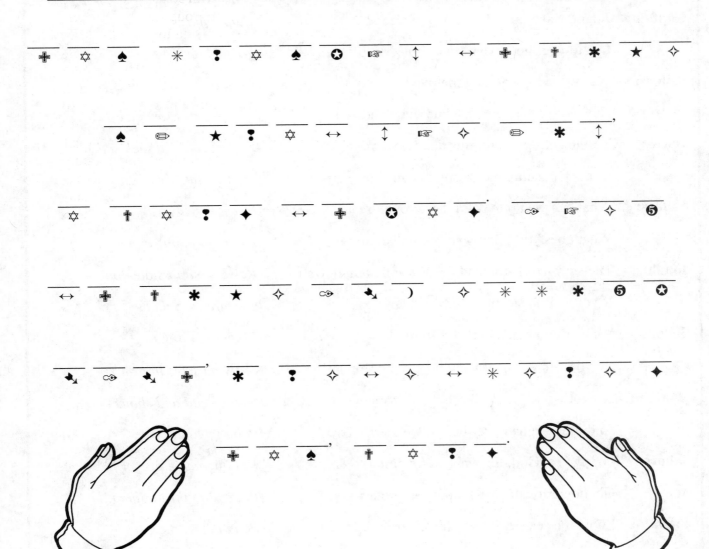

Jonah Action Rhyme

Directions: Divide students into three groups: Jonah, the captain, and the sailors. Have them read the parts to one another and do the actions. The story is found in Jonah 1–2.

Jonah:	God wants me in Nineveh; I just can't go there!	*(Shake head "no" and look scared.)*
	I'll get on this ship and get some nice sea air.	*(Point and walk in place.)*
Captain:	Welcome aboard! The weather is fine.	*(Extend arms in welcome.)*
	We'll have a smooth trip and be there on time!	*(Point to watch.)*
Sailors:	Oh no, what's this? The sea's getting rough.	*(Sway back and forth.)*
	We'll sink if we don't start throwing out some stuff.	*(Pretend to throw things.)*
Captain:	Jonah, wake up! How can you sleep?	*(Clap hands.)*
	Cry to your god; we're in trouble, deep!	*(Wring hands.)*
Sailors:	We've tried everything that we know to do,	*(Hold head with hands.)*
	Now we've cast the lots, and they landed on you.	*(Pretend to throw dice.)*
Jonah:	Yes, it's all my fault, this danger we're in.	*(Hang head and look sad.)*
	God's punishing me because of my sin.	*(Point to heaven, then yourself.)*
Sailors:	What can we do to calm these rough seas?	*(Sway roughly.)*
	What does your God want? Can you tell us, please?	*(Hold out hands imploringly.)*
Jonah:	The storm will stop and the sea will calm down	*(Raise hand in stop motion.)*
	If you will throw me overboard now.	*(Gesture with thumb.)*
Sailors:	We can't do that! Let's try to row!	*(Pretend to row.)*
	Maybe our strong arms will help the ship go.	*(Show muscles in arm.)*
Captain:	It's not working, men! Lay your oars down	*(Shake head and shout.)*
	And throw Jonah over before we all drown!	*(Point to Jonah.)*
Sailors:	Forgive us, God, for what we're going to do.	*(Hold hands in prayer.)*
	Goodbye, Jonah. May your god protect you.	*(Pretend to throw Jonah.)*
Captain:	Look, the sea's calm and it's clear in the south.	*(Point down, then up.)*
	And Jonah just went inside that fish's mouth!	*(Point and look surprised.)*

Bible Story Acrostic

Directions: Jonah had a problem with something. What was it? To find out, use the clues from the story in Jonah 1 to fill in the words of the acrostic. Look up the Bible verses if you need help.

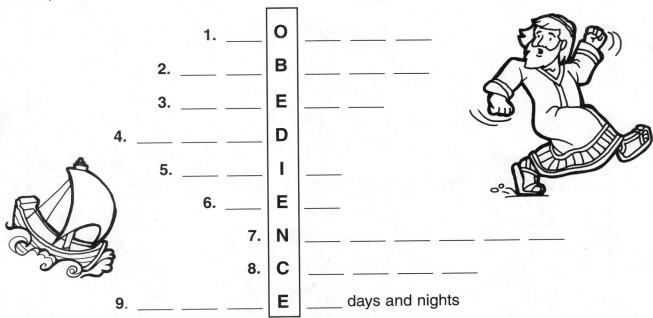

1. ___ __O__ ___ ___
2. ___ ___ __B__ ___ ___
3. ___ ___ __E__ ___ ___
4. ___ ___ __D__ ___
5. ___ ___ __I__ ___
6. ___ __E__ ___
7. __N__ ___ ___ ___ ___
8. __C__ ___ ___ ___ ___
9. ___ ___ ___ __E__ ___ days and nights

CLUES

1. Where Jonah went (Jonah 1:3)

2. Who Jonah told the sailors he was (Jonah 1:9)

3. What Jonah did during the storm (Jonah 1:5)

4. What God sent (Jonah 1:4)

5. What Jonah got on (Jonah 1:3)

6. To stop the storm, the sailors threw Jonah into this. (Jonah 1:12, 15)

7. Where God told Jonah to go (Jonah 1:2)

8. What the sailors threw over to try to save the ship (Jonah 1:5)

9. How long Jonah was in the fish God sent to swallow him (Jonah 1:17)

Obedience Song

Directions: Sing the song. Then answer the questions.

(Tune: "B-I-N-G-O")

God told Jonah where to go, but Jonah ran away.

He did not obey,

He did not obey,

He did not obey.

He tried to run away.

God prepared a great big fish to swallow Jonah whole.

Jonah prayed to God,

Jonah prayed to God,

Jonah prayed to God

And said, "Yes, I will go."

God's Word tells me where to go and just what I should do.

I'll obey God's Word,

I'll obey God's Word,

I'll obey God's Word.

Yes, Lord, I'll follow You!

Questions

God told Jonah what He wanted him to do. How does God tell us what He wants us to do?

_____

How can people tell whether or not you love God? (Read John 14:21.)

_____

Why is it sometimes hard to obey God? _____

_____

Jonah in the Sea Mobile

Make this mobile to hang it in your room as a reminder of the lesson in obedience that God taught Jonah.

Materials

- patterns (pages 11 and 12)
- poster board (blue or white)
- cardstock
- crayons or colored markers
- scissors
- hole punch
- string or thread
- stapler and staples

Finished Product

Directions

1. Copy the patterns below and on page 12 on heavy paper such as cardstock.
2. Color the patterns and cut them out.
3. Cut out a strip of poster board about 3" x 24". If you are using white poster board, color blue waves to represent the sea. (*Optional:* Cut the top of the strip to look like waves.)
4. Staple the two ends of the poster board strip together to make a circle.
5. Punch a hole in the top of each pattern. Punch holes in the bottom of the poster board circle, spaced equally along its length.
6. Cut five pieces of string of various lengths. Tie one in each of the holes in the poster board circle.
7. Tie the other end of each string to one of the patterns.
8. Punch three holes in the top of the poster board circle, equally spaced out.
9. Tie three pieces of string of equal length in the three holes. Tie them together to make a hanger for the mobile.

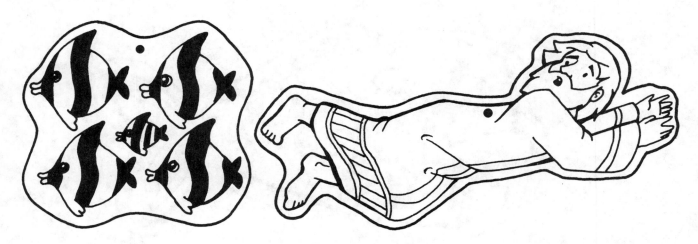

Jonah in the Sea Mobile

See page 11 for directions.

Jesus Talks About Jonah

Directions: Hundreds of years after Jonah lived, Jesus spoke of him to His disciples. Use the letters from the number/letter box to complete what Jesus said. The first letter is done for you to show you how it works.

	5	6	7	8	9
1	A	E	R	I	F
2	J	U	B	Y	S
3	M	O	V	L	H
4	G	T	W	N	D

AS J
    2-5 3-6 4-8 1-5 3-9   4-7 1-5 2-9   4-6 3-9 1-7 1-6 1-6

    4-9 1-5 2-8 2-9   1-5 4-8 4-9   4-8 1-8 4-5 3-9 4-6 2-9

IN THE ___ ___ ___ ___ ___ OF A ___ ___ ___ ___ ___ ___ ___ ___ ,
       2-7 1-6 3-8 3-8 2-8   3-9 2-6 4-5 1-6   1-9 1-8 2-9 3-9

SO THE ___ ___ ___ OF ___ ___ ___ ___ ___ ___ ___ ___ ___
       2-9 3-6 4-8   3-5 1-5 4-8   4-7 1-8 3-8 3-8   2-7 1-6

    4-6 3-9 1-7 1-6 1-6   4-9 1-5 2-8 2-9   1-5 4-8 4-9

    4-8 1-8 4-5 3-9 4-6 2-9   IN THE ___ ___ ___ ___ ___
                           3-9 1-6 1-5 1-7 4-6

OF THE ___ ___ ___ ___ ___ . (Matthew 12:40)
       1-6 1-5 1-7 4-6 3-9

Discussion: What do you think Jesus was talking about?

Who Was Jonah?

Directions: Find and circle the words from the Bible story of Jonah in the word search puzzle. Then, write the leftover letters in order on the lines below to discover how Jonah described himself.

I	A	S	A	I	L	O	R	S	M	O
A	N	H	P	E	B	R	E	T	W	V
A	N	I	D	I	T	H	R	O	W	E
W	H	O	N	R	A	S	H	R	I	R
S	P	T	H	E	E	L	O	M	R	B
D	T	H	S	E	V	G	O	D	O	O
F	H	E	A	V	E	E	H	N	W	A
H	C	O	M	A	D	S	H	E	T	R
H	A	F	R	A	I	D	E	S	E	D
A	L	A	N	F	D	T	H	E	L	A
N	M	T	A	R	S	H	I	S	H	D

Word list:

NINEVEH
TARSHISH
SHIP
STORM
AFRAID
SEA
THROW
OVERBOARD
SAILORS
CALM
FISH

Jonah told the sailors, "____ ____ ____ ____ ____ ____ ____

____ ____ ____ ____ ____ ____ ____ ____

____ ____ ____ ____, ____ ____ ____ ____ ____ ____

____ ____ ____ ____, ____ ____ ____ ____ ____ ____

____ ____ ____ ____ ____ ____ ____ ____

____ ____ ____ ____." (Jonah 1:9)

After the Storm

Directions: Jonah told the sailors on the ship that the sea would calm down if they threw him overboard. They didn't want to do such a terrible thing to him! But they finally decided it was the only way to save the ship and the people on it. What happened after they threw him overboard? Use the letter/number code to discover what the sailors did.

A	B	C	D	E	F	G	H	I	J	K	L	M
6	5	4	3	2	1	0	9	8	7	10	11	12

N	O	P	Q	R	S	T	U	V	W	X	Y	Z
20	19	18	17	16	15	14	13	26	25	24	23	22

THEN THEY TOOK JONAH AND THREW HIM OVERBOARD, AND

THE RAGING SEA GREW CALM. AT THIS THE MEN

___ ___ ___ ___ ___ ___ ___ ___ ___ ___ ___ ___ ___
 0 16   2   6 14 11 23   1   2   6 16   2   3

___ ___ ___ ___ ___ ___ ___ , AND
14   9   2 11 19 16   3

___ ___ ___ ___ ___ ___ ___ ___ ___ ___ ___ ___
14   9   2 23 19   1   1   2 16   2   3   6

___ ___ ___ ___ ___ ___ ___ ___ ___ ___ ___ ___ ___
15   6   4 16   8   1   8   4   2 14 19 14   9   2

___ ___ ___ ___ AND ___ ___ ___ ___ ___ ___ ___ ___
11 19 16   3   12   6   3   2 26 19 25 15

TO HIM. (Jonah 1:15–16)

What Jonah Did

Directions: Jonah was thrown overboard during a storm at sea. He probably thought he was going to drown, but God had other plans for his prophet. God sent a big fish to swallow Jonah whole. It didn't kill Jonah, but it made him think. What did he do the three days and nights he was inside the stomach of the fish? To find out, cross out all these letters on the fish: **B, F, J, I, O**. Write the remaining letters in order on the lines.

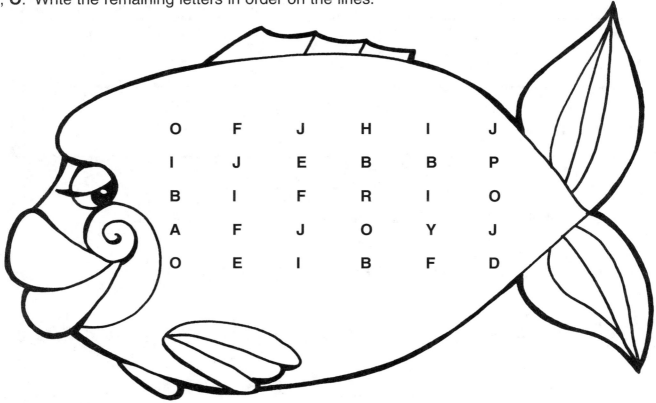

What did Jonah do inside the fish?

____ ____   ____ ____ ____ ____ ____ ____ .

What would you do if you had been Jonah?

_____

_____

_____

Send Up the Fish!

Directions: God had a plan for Jonah, and it wasn't for him to drown. He sent a big fish to save Jonah. Help the fish find its way up from the bottom of the sea to Jonah. Read what happened in Jonah 1–2.

FINISH

START

God in Charge Crossword

Directions: Use the clues below to figure out the words that complete the crossword puzzle. **A** words go across; **D** words go down. Look up the Bible verses if you need help.

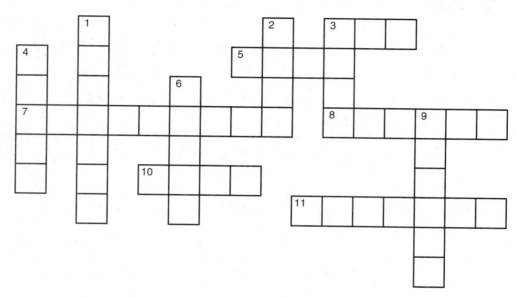

Jonah tried to run from God, but God saw everything he did. He was in charge the whole time.

1-D   Where God told Jonah to go (Jonah 1:2)

8-A   What God wanted Jonah to do in that city (Jonah 1:2)

3-D   What God saw Jonah get on (Jonah 1:3)

2-D and 4-D   What God sent to stop Jonah (Jonah 1:4)

9-D   How the sailors felt when the weather got bad (Jonah 1:5)

11-A   Who woke Jonah up and told him to pray for help (Jonah 1:6)

6-D   When the sailors cast lots to see who was causing the storm, God made the lot fall on him. (Jonah 1:7)

7-A   Where the sailors threw Jonah (Jonah 1:15)

3-A and 10-A   When Jonah hit the water, the _____ became _____. (Jonah 1:15)

5-A   What God sent to save Jonah from drowning (Jonah 1:17)

What Happened When?

Directions: Look at the pictures carefully. In the boxes, number the pictures from 1 to 6 to show the order in which they happened. If you need help, read the story in Jonah 1–2.

Memory Verse Fish Craft

Materials

- patterns on page 21
- two paper plates (or 6½" poster board circles)
- scissors
- crayons or colored markers
- hole punch

- construction paper
- glue
- stapler and staples
- string

Directions

1. Holding the two paper plates (or circles) front to front, cut out a section for the fish's mouth.

2. Color the two plates or circles.

3. Copy the patterns on page 21 on construction paper.

4. Color the patterns and cut them.

5. Glue the tail and top and bottom fins in place on the inside of one of the saucers or circles.

6. Holding the paper plates or circles, front to front, staple them together all around the rims. Do not staple the mouth area.

7. Glue the eyes on the fish on both sides above the mouth. Glue a small fin to each side.

8. Cut out the memory verse card. Punch a hole through the top of the memory verse card. Then tie a piece of string to it.

9. Read the memory verse; then, place it in the fish's mouth. Retrieve it carefully by pulling the string.

The Lord your God is with you,
he is mighty to save.
(Zephaniah 3:17a)

Memory Verse Card

Finished Product

Memory Verse Fish Craft

See page 20 for directions.

Eyes

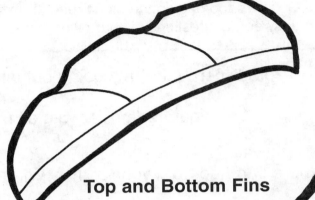

Top and Bottom Fins

Tail

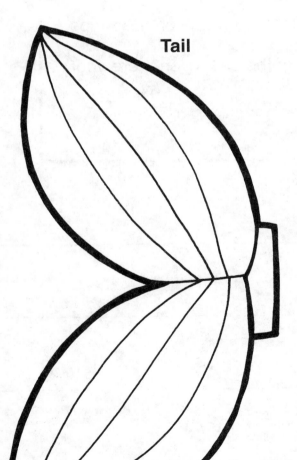

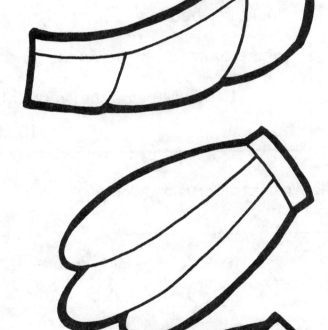

Side Fins

David's Words for Jonah

Directions: Many years before Jonah was born, David wrote a psalm about why no one can run from God. It's too bad Jonah didn't read it! Read the verses in the box from David's psalm. Then answer the questions in your own words.

> You discern (see) my going out and my lying down;
>
> you are familiar with all my ways.
>
> Where can I go from your Spirit? Where can I flee (run) from your presence? If I go up to the heavens, you are there; if I make my bed in the depths, you are there. If I rise on the wings of the dawn, if I settle on the far side of the sea, even there your hand will guide me, your right hand will hold me fast.
>
> (Psalm 139:3, 7–10)

1. What does God know about you?

_____

2. Where can you go to get away from God?

_____

3. How does this truth about God make you feel?

_____

4. When might these verses make you afraid?

_____

5. When might you be glad to remember these verses?

_____

A Rough Ride

Jonah got on a ship headed in the opposite direction from where God told him to go. Jonah probably didn't expect it to be such a rough ride. God sent a storm that put everyone on the ship in danger until Jonah decided to obey. Follow the directions to make a picture of Jonah's rough ride. You can read the story in Jonah 1.

Materials

- patterns on pages 23 and 24
- scissors
- craft stick for each student
- crayons or markers
- glue

Directions

1. Color the picture of the stormy sea on page 24.

2. Carefully cut a slit where the line is on the sea.

3. Color and cut out the ship below.

4. Glue the ship to a craft stick for a handle.

5. Push the ship through the slit on the picture and move it back and forth for a rough ride on the stormy sea as you sing the song.

Finished Product

God Is With Me Song

(*Tune:* "Skip to My Lou")

God is with me every day,

Close beside me all the way.

Even on a stormy sea,

I know that God's with me.

A Rough Ride

Follow the directions on page 23.

Jonah's Attitude

Directions: When Jonah got on a ship headed for Tarshish, he had an attitude of rebellion toward God. When he prayed inside the fish that had swallowed him, his attitude had changed. What was his attitude? To find out, solve the clues. Then, write the clue answers on the matching numbered lines.

Clues

_____ 1. You can find me in *shot* but not in *spot*.

_____ 2. I am in the middle of *pat* but not in *put*.

_____ 3. I am first in *short* and last in *lips*.

_____ 4. I am the letter you use to talk about yourself.

_____ 5. I am first in *today* and last in *night*.

_____ 6. You can find me in both *glove* and *grass*.

_____ 7. I appear twice in *noon* and *morning*.

_____ 8. I am in *vase* but not in *base*.

_____ 9. You can see me in *crack* but you won't find me in *crab*.

Jonah had an attitude of

____ ____ ____ ____ ____ ____ ____ ____ ____ ____ ____ ____
  5   1   2   7   9   3   6   4   8   4   7   6

What made Jonah change his attitude? _____

_____

_____

Where Were They?

Directions: Match the characters and things in the Bible story in Jonah 1–2 to the places where they were. Some were in more than one place. Read the story to check your answers.

_____ 1. God

_____ 2. Jonah

_____ 3. Sailors

_____ 4. Fish

_____ 5. Cargo

A. Joppa

B. Ship

C. Sea

D. Fish

E. Dry Ground

Jonah Fingerplay

Materials

- patterns below
- clear tape
- scissors
- crayons or colored markers

Directions

1. Color the Jonah and fish finger puppets below.

2. Cut out the finger puppets. Be sure to cut out the tabs as part of the puppets.

3. Tape the tabs together to make the puppets fit on your fingers.

4. Put a finger puppet on each hand and act out the rhyme as you say it.

Fingerplay Rhyme

Down, down, down,

Jonah went into the sea,

Crying out to God,

"Please, save me!"

Swish, swish, swish,

A fish came swimming by

And swallowed Jonah whole,

For the Lord had heard his cry.

Jonah Finger Puppet

Fish Finger Puppet

Jonah Prays–God Answers

Directions: For three days and nights Jonah lived inside a fish, and oh how he prayed! Did God answer his prayers? To find out, follow the directions.

1. Cross out every word in the boxes that . . .
   - ends with the letter **S**
   - begins with the letter **G**
   - rhymes with the word *your*
2. Write the remaining words in order on the lines.

AND	GOD	THE	HIS	GIVE
LORD	PRAYS	GO	COMMANDED	MORE
FOUR	THE	FISH	DOOR	AND
IT	YES	VOMITED	JONAH	DAYS
POOR	ONTO	CROSS	DRY	LAND

_____ _____ _____

_____ _____ _____ ,

_____ _____ _____

_____ . (Jonah 2:10)

Jonah Goes to Nineveh

(Based on Jonah 3:1–4:11)

Jonah was on dry ground again after living inside a big fish for three days and nights! God spoke to him a second time and said, "Go to the great city of Nineveh and proclaim to it the message I give you." This time Jonah did not try to run away but headed for Nineveh.

The city of Nineveh was a big place with about 120,000 people living there. It was the center of the nation of Assyria. The Assyrians were famous for their cruelty and wickedness. No wonder Jonah hadn't wanted to go there! But God loved the people of Assyria and of Nineveh, and he wanted to give them one last chance to accept Him. Jonah's job was to go throughout the big city, giving everyone God's message: "Forty more days and Nineveh will be overturned."

The people of Nineveh listened to Jonah's words of warning. The king of Nineveh was so sad when he heard what Jonah had to say, he took off his beautiful, royal robes, put on ugly sackcloth (a rough, uncomfortable material), and sat down in the dust. That was the way people in those times showed sorrow. The king made a decree and made sure everyone in the city knew about it:

> *Do not let any man or beast,*
> *herd or flock, taste anything; do*
> *not let them eat or drink. But*
> *let man and beast be covered*
> *with sackcloth. Let everyone*
> *call urgently on God. Let them*
> *give up their evil ways and*
> *their violence. Who knows?*
> *God may yet relent and with*
> *compassion turn from his fierce*
> *anger so that we will not perish.*

The people obeyed the king's orders. The whole city repented and fasted to show how sorry they were for their sin. God had compassion on them and did not destroy the city after all.

Of course, God already knew the people would repent and turn to Him, but Jonah did not. He was angry when he saw that God was not going to destroy the people. Jonah said to God, "Isn't this what I said You would do?" Instead of being happy that the people of Nineveh had turned to God, Jonah was upset. He asked God to take his life because he didn't want to live any longer.

Wasn't Jonah being silly and stubborn? He should have been thrilled that God had used him to save a whole city of lost people. But Jonah was thinking only of himself. He went out to a place east of the city, built himself a little shelter from the sun, and sat down to watch the city, hoping that God would destroy it after all. God had compassion on His prophet and made a vine grow up next to the shelter to provide more shade from the hot sun. Jonah was happy to have more shade, but when a worm came and killed the vine, he began to feel depressed again.

"I am angry enough to die!" Jonah said. God scolded him for his selfish attitude. God said, "You are more concerned about the vine dying than you are about the 120,000 lost people in Nineveh!" It was a sad ending to Jonah's story. He started out with an attitude of rebellion and disobedience. After God taught him a "fishy" lesson, Jonah had an attitude of thankfulness and obedience. Now Jonah had an attitude of selfishness. He did not care about the people of Nineveh. Fortunately, God did.

What Happened in Nineveh

Directions: God told Jonah a second time to go to Nineveh. This time Jonah obeyed. What happened when he got there? Underline the correct words to complete each sentence. Read the story in Jonah 3 if you need help.

1. Jonah walked through the city saying,

   a. "Forty more days and Nineveh will be overturned."

   b. "God offers you mercy if you will receive him."

   c. "God loves you and has a wonderful plan for your life."

2. The people of Nineveh

   a. refused to listen to Jonah.

   b. made fun of Jonah.

   c. listened to Jonah and believed God.

3. The king of Nineveh

   a. arrested Jonah and put him in jail.

   b. put on sackcloth and sat in the dust.

   c. invited Jonah to dinner.

4. The king ordered the people of Nineveh to

   a. call on God and give up their evil ways.

   b. be nice to Jonah.

   c. ignore Jonah and he would go away.

5. When God saw the people's response, He

   a. destroyed the city with fire.

   b. had compassion on them and did not destroy the city.

   c. told Jonah to preach to them again.

What does this story teach us about God? Read Psalm 116:5 if you need a hint.

Nineveh Repents

Directions: Complete the poem with words from the box. If you need help, read the story in Jonah 3:6–10.

dead	free
dust	say
do	pray

The king of Nineveh was sitting on his throne one day

When he heard of Jonah and what he had to _____.

Did the king get angry? Did he yell and fuss?

No! He just took off his robe and sat down in the _____.

He made a proclamation for his people to obey.

"Everyone must fast," he said, "and everyone should _____."

"Give up your evil ways right now and turn to God," he said.

"Maybe God will change his mind. If He won't, we're _____!"

Everyone in Nineveh obeyed the king's decree.

That day the people turned to God, and it set the city _____.

God showed them compassion as only God can _____.

No one was destroyed, for the people's repentance was true.

Jonah in Nineveh Puzzle

Directions: Color the picture pieces and then cut them out. Fit them together to form a picture of Jonah preaching in Nineveh. Read Jonah 3:6–10 to find out what the people did after they heard his message.

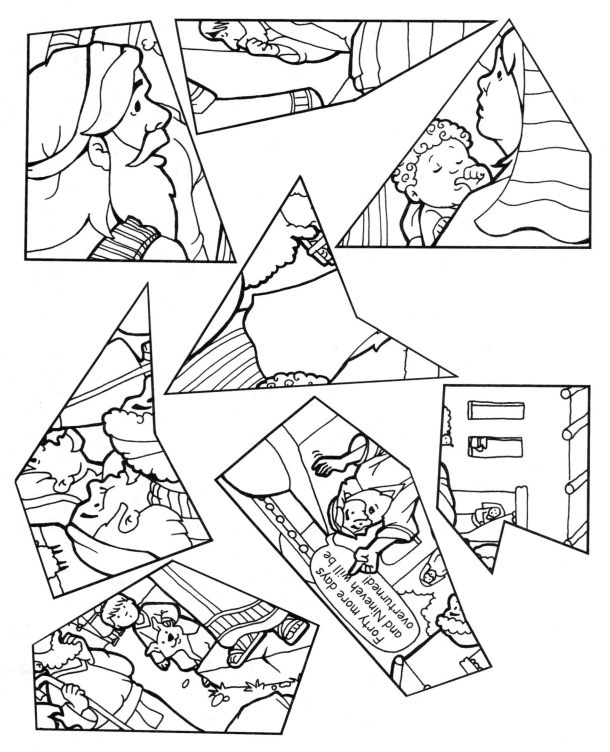

Saved!

Directions: Complete the sentences about Jonah in Nineveh; then, circle the words in the puzzle. Look up the Bible verses to check your answers. Write the leftover letters in order on the lines to discover what saved the people of Nineveh.

K	I	N	G	T	H	C
E	R	I	N	I	N	O
C	O	N	E	V	D	M
A	B	E	I	E	T	P
L	E	V	Y	E	S	A
L	S	E	B	T	E	S
E	B	H	S	L	V	S
O	I	A	E	V	I	I
E	F	D	G	O	L	O
D	F	O	R	T	Y	N

1. God said to Jonah a second time, "Go to _____." (Jonah 3:2)

2. This time Jonah _____. (Jonah 3:3)

3. Jonah's message from God was: "_____ more days and Nineveh will be overturned." (Jonah 3:4)

4. The people declared a _____, which means they stopped eating, to show that they were sorry for their sins. (Jonah 3:5)

5. The _____ took off his royal _____, put on sackcloth, and sat in the dust. (Jonah 3:6)

6. He decreed that all his people should _____ on God and give up their

   _____ ways. (Jonah 3:8)

7. When God saw that the people were truly sorry for their sins, He had

   _____ on them and did not destroy the city. (Jonah 3:10)

What saved the people?

____ ____ ____ ____ ____ ____ ____ ____ ____ ____ ____ ____ ____

____ ____ ____ ____ ____ ____ ____ ____ ____ ____ ____. (Jonah 3:5)

In What Order?

Directions: Look at the pictures carefully. Number them from 1 to 6 to show the order in which they happened. If you need help, read the complete story in Jonah 3–4.

Compassion Door Hanging

Make this door hanging as a reminder of the compassion God showed to Jonah, to the people of Nineveh, and for the compassion He shows to you every day.

Materials

- tape
- word cards below
- patterns on page 36
- crayons or colored markers
- construction paper strip (3" wide x 16" long)

- string
- scissors
- corregated cardboard
- glue

Directions

1. Cut a V-shaped notch in the the bottom of the 3" 16" construction paper strip as shown.

2. Cut out the heart patterns on page 36 and the word cards below.

3. Cut four one-inch squares from the corregated cardboard.

4. Glue a cardboard square to the back of each heart.

5. Glue the word cards and hearts on the paper strip as shown to the right. (The cardboard squares will make the hearts stick out a bit for a three-dimensional look.)

6. Decorate the hanging with colorful designs and squiggles.

7. Tape a piece of string to the back of the hanging so you can hang it on your door at home.

Finished Product

x

The LORD is	and	and
		Psalm 145:8

Compassion Door Hanging

See page 35 for directions for patterns below.

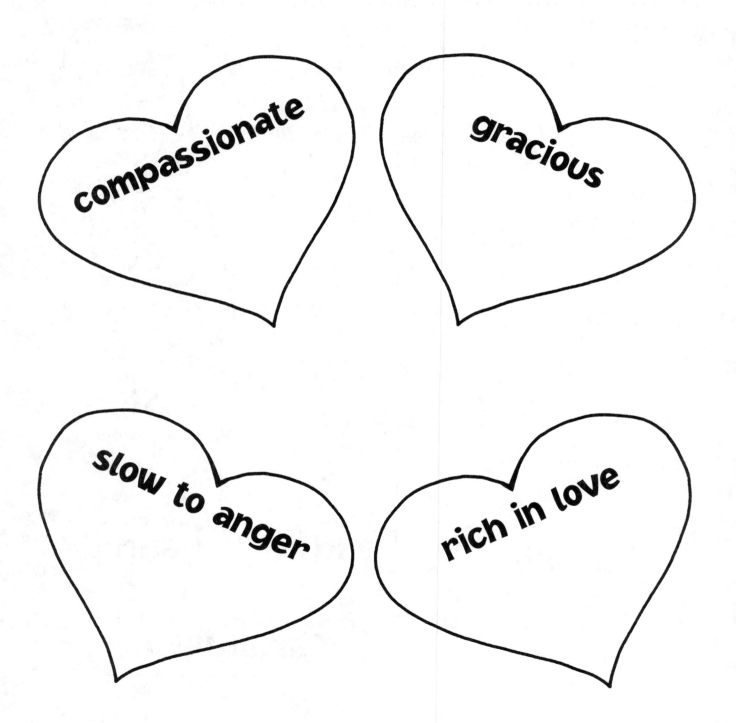

36

"God Is" Song

Directions: Jonah told God He was "gracious and compassionate, slow to anger and abounding in love" (Jonah 4:2). But Jonah was angry with God for being all those good things! Jonah's selfish anger really had him mixed up. Sing this song to praise God for those good things.

(Tune: "Old MacDonald Had a Farm")

God is everything we need, and I love Him so.

Gracious and compassionate,

That's why I love Him so.

He forgives the wrong I do

And He will forgive you too.

God is everything we need, and I love Him so.

God is everything we need, and I love Him so.

Slow to anger; that's my God!

That's why I love Him so.

Though I sometimes disobey,

He's patient with me day by day.

God is everything we need, and I love Him so.

God is everything we need and I love Him so.

He loves me more than anyone.

That's why I love Him so.

Nothing we can ever do

Will change His love for me and you.

God is everything we need, and I love Him so.

What are some other "good things" about God that make you love Him?

_____

_____

Bad Attitude–Good Attitude

Directions: God didn't do what Jonah wanted, and Jonah got angry. When God tried to talk to him about it, Jonah argued, then sat down and pouted. Jonah definitely had a bad attitude! What kind of attitude should Jonah have had? The same attitude God wants you to have. Decode the words to complete the Bible verse and find out what your attitude (and Jonah's) should be.

A	C	D	E	G	H
3×3	$5 + 2$	$10 - 4$	4×4	$8 - 5$	$9 - 4$
I	**K**	**L**	**M**	**N**	**O**
5×2	$11 - 9$	$7 + 4$	$12 - 8$	$5 + 3$	3×4
P	**S**	**T**	**U**	**Y**	
5×3	$10 - 9$	$7 + 7$	9×2	$27 - 10$	

Therefore, as God's chosen people, holy and dearly loved,

clothe yourselves with

__ __ __ __ __ __ __ __ __ __ ,
7 12 4 15 9 1 1 10 12 8

__ __ __ __ __ __ __ __ ,
2 10 8 6 8 16 1 1

__ __ __ __ __ __ __ __ ,
5 18 4 10 11 10 14 17

__ __ __ __ __ __ __ __ __ __ and
3 16 8 14 11 16 8 16 1 1

__ __ __ __ __ __ __ __ .
15 9 14 10 16 8 7 16

(Colossians 3:12)

Jonah Crossword

Directions: Read the clues about Jonah. Write the correct words in the crossword puzzle to complete Jonah's story found in Jonah 4. **A** words go across; **D** words go down.

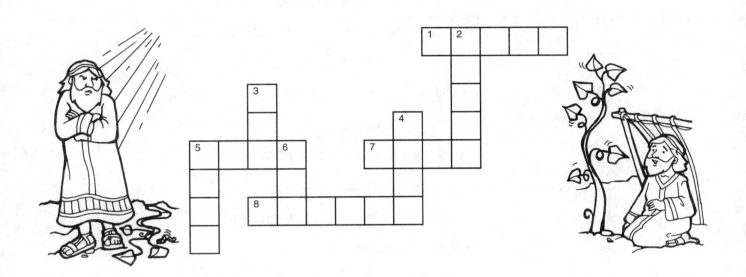

2-D   How Jonah felt when God did not destroy Nineveh (Jonah 4:1)

6-D   Jonah was so upset, he told God he just wanted to _____. (Jonah 4:3)

7-A   Jonah went out and sat down to watch the _____ to see what would happen. He was probably hoping God would destroy it even though He had said He wouldn't. (Jonah 4:5)

4-D   Jonah built himself a shelter. He was happy when God made a _____ grow up to give him more shade. (Jonah 4:6)

5-D   But the next day a _____ chewed on the vine and it died. (Jonah 4:7)

5-A and 3-D   God sent a very hot _____ and as the _____ beat down on Jonah, he was miserable. (Jonah 4:8)

1-A   With little shade from the heat, Jonah became _____ and he complained to God. (Jonah 4:8)

8-A   God scolded Jonah for caring more about the vine and his own comfort than he did for the _____ of Nineveh. (Jonah 4:10–11)

Compassion Rap

(Based on Jonah 4)

God said, "Jonah, what's wrong with you?

Don't you care about anybody but you?

The message you preached made the people repent.

Now they're saved! That's why you were sent."

But Jonah didn't care, not for a minute.

He obeyed the Lord, but his heart wasn't in it.

God wants us to C-A-R-E

The way He cares about you and me.

He has compassion on me and you,

And He wants us to show compassion, too.

To care about people—that's why we're here,

To help and encourage and calm their fears.

To share the love of God wherever we are,

Whoever we're with—to be a shining star!

With a smile on our face and a tender heart,

We can make a difference if we do our part.

Jonah didn't get it—how about you?

Do you understand what God wants you to do?

Care about people—that's all there is to it.

Show some compassion. Go on, just do it!

What are some practical ways we can show God's compassion to people? _____

_____

Compassion Bookmark

Follow the directions to make a bookmark to remind you that God wants you to show compassion. Keep the bookmark in your Bible in the story of Jonah. Read Jonah 3–4 to find out how God showed compassion, but Jonah didn't.

Materials

- bookmark pattern
- cardstock
- crayons or colored markers
- scissors
- hole punch
- ribbon or yarn (about 25" long)
- tape
- heart stickers

Directions

1. Copy the bookmark on cardstock and decorate it with crayons or markers and heart stickers.

2. Cut the bookmark out.

3. Use a hole punch to punch holes in all the circles.

4. Put tape around one end of the ribbon or yarn.

5. Poke the taped end of the ribbon or yarn through one of the top holes.

6. You may want to tape the loose end on the back of the bookmark to hold it. (Leave about 4" on the end for tying a bow when you're done.)

7. Weave the ribbon or yarn in and out of the holes all around the bookmark.

8. When you get to the last hole at the top, untape the ribbon or yarn from the back and tie the two ends together in a bow.

Compassion is the fashion for the Christian every day!

"Be kind and compassionate to one another." (Ephesians 4:32a)

"Each of you should look not only to your own interests, but also to the interests of others." (Philippians 2:4)

God's Mercy

Directions: We all sin and deserve to be punished. But God doesn't always give us what we deserve. God made a promise, through the Old Testament prophet Jeremiah, to those who repent of their sins. Write the numbered words in order on the lines below to discover His promise. How did God keep this promise to Nineveh?

If 1	I 22	evil 27	uprooted 13	planned 40
that 7	any 3	disaster 37	its 26	of 25
had 39	relent 30	down 15	announce 6	I 28
warned 23	destroyed 17	I 5	will 29	it 35
and 16	inflict 33	the 36	time 4	nation or kingdom 9
nation 21	I 38	torn 14	a 8	not 32
at 2	and 31	that 20	repents 24	to 11
is 10	on 34	and 18	if 19	be 12

____ ____ ____ ____ ____
1   2   3   4   5

____ ____ ____ ____
6   7   8   9

____ ____ ____ ____ , ____
10   11   12   13   14

____ ____ ____ , ____
15   16   17   18

____ ____ ____ ____ ____
19   20   21   22   23

____ ____ ____ ____ , then ____
24   25   26   27   28

____ ____ ____ ____
29   30   31   32

____ ____ ____ ____
33   34   35   36

____ ____ ____ ____ .
37   38   39   40

(Jeremiah 18:7–8)

Jonah Paper Bag Puppet

Make this puppet. Then, use it to make Jonah say the rap on page 44.

Materials

- paper lunch bag
- patterns on this page
- scissors
- crayons or colored markers
- glue

Directions

1. Color and cut out the patterns.

2. Glue the head to the bottom of the paper bag.

3. Glue the mouth and neck under the bottom flap of the bag.

4. Put your hand in the bag and move the mouth to make Jonah talk.

Finished Product

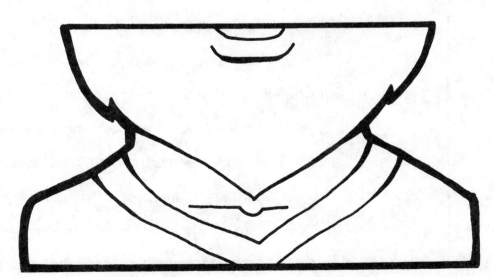

Jonah Puppet Rap

Directions: Use your Jonah puppet, page 43, to say this rap, summarizing Jonah's story.

My name is Jonah and I'm sorry to say

I disobeyed God and tried to run away.

I got on a ship to hide from Him,

But the next thing I knew I was taking a swim!

When a storm hit the ship, the sailors took me

And threw me overboard into the sea.

I thought I'd die; that was my wish,

But instead I was swallowed by a great big fish!

I knew I was safely in God's hand.

I prayed, and that fish threw me up on dry land.

This time I did what the Lord said to do.

I'd learned my lesson. Well, wouldn't you?

I warned the people of Nineveh town

That God would destroy it, right down to the ground.

But when the king and his people repented and prayed,

God had compassion and the city was saved.

That made me mad 'cause I didn't care

About any of the people living there.

The Lord scolded me, I'm ashamed to say;

I had to learn another lesson that day.

Jonah Picture Booklet

Directions

1. Color the pictures below and on page 46.
2. Cut out the pages on the solid lines.
3. Fold them on the broken lines.
4. Put the pages in numbered order.
5. Staple the pages together at the left edge.
6. Tell the story by looking at the pictures.

"This is love for God: to obey his commands."

(1 John 5:3a)

11

Jonah Learns to Obey

(Jonah 1–4)

_____
(name)

9

TO JOPPA

2

7

4

Jonah Picture Booklet

Follow the directions on page 45.

Answer Key

Page 7

YOU BROUGHT MY LIFE UP FROM THE PIT, O LORD MY GOD. WHEN MY LIFE WAS EBBING AWAY, I REMEMBERED YOU, LORD.

Page 9

1. JOPPA   3. SLEPT   5. SHIP
                                6. SEA
2. HEBREW   4. WIND   7. NINEVEH

Jonah had a problem with OBEDIENCE.

Page 13

AS <u>JONAH WAS THREE DAYS AND NIGHTS</u> IN THE <u>BELLY</u> OF A <u>HUGE FISH</u>, SO THE <u>SON</u> OF <u>MAN WILL BE THREE DAYS AND NIGHTS</u> IN THE <u>HEART</u> OF THE <u>EARTH</u>.
(Matthew 12:40)

Page 14

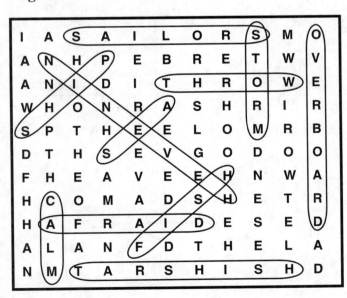

Jonah told the sailors, "<u>I AM A HEBREW AND I WORSHIP THE LORD, THE GOD OF HEAVEN, WHO MADE THE SEA AND THE LAND</u>."
(Jonah 1:9)

Page 15

THEN THEY TOOK JONAH AND THREW HIM OVERBOARD, AND THE RAGING SEA GREW CALM. AT THIS THE MEN <u>GREATLY FEARED THE LORD</u>, AND <u>THEY OFFERED A SACRIFICE TO THE LORD</u> AND <u>MADE VOWS</u> TO HIM. (Jonah 1:15–16)

Page 16

HE PRAYED.

Page 17

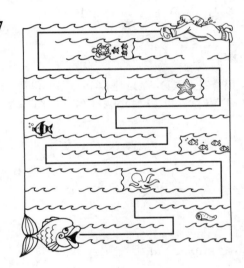

Page 18

(crossword)

Page 19

2   5
4   6
1   3

Answer Key

Page 22

1. everything
2. nowhere
3. Answers will vary.
4. Answers will vary.
5. Answers will vary.

Page 25

thanksgiving

Page 26

1. A, B, C, D, E
2. A, B, C, D, E
3. B
4. C
5. B, C

Page 28

AND THE LORD COMMANDED THE FISH, AND IT VOMITED JONAH ONTO DRY LAND.

Page 30

1. a
2. c
3. b
4. a
5. b

Page 31

say, dust, pray, dead, free, do

Page 32

Page 33

1. Nineveh
2. obeyed
3. Forty
4. fast
5. king, robes
6. call, evil
7. compassion

The Ninevites believed God.

Page 34

2	6
1	4
3	5

Page 38

compassion, kindness, humility, gentleness and patience

Page 39

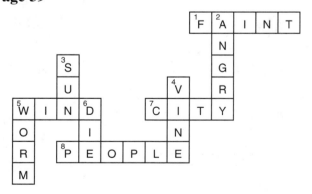

Page 42

If at any time I announce that a nation or kingdom is to be uprooted, torn down and destroyed, and if that nation I warned repents of its evil, **then** I will relent and not inflict on it the disaster I had planned.